Reigning While It's Raining

A Woman's Journey Towards Her Destiny

Reigning While It's Raining:
A Woman's Journey Towards Her Destiny
By
Lishala Thomas-Carter

Published by Greater Works Enterprises
www.greaterworksenterprises.com
2020

Copyright © 2020 by Lishala Thomas-Carter

All rights reserved. This book or any portion thereof may not be reproduced or used in any manner whatsoever without the express written permission of the publisher except for the use of brief quotations in a book review or scholarly journal.

First Printing: 2020

ISBN 978-0-9975643-8-9

Greater Works Enterprises
Website: www.greaterworksenterprises.com

This book is dedicated to my beloved grandmother.

The ultimate, original Purpose Pusher.

Baby Girl is finally waking up!

Table of Contents

Introduction ix
Chapter 1 – I Can't Get My Hair Wet 1
Chapter 2 – How I See Me.. 7
Chapter 3 – Go Against the Grain.. 13
Chapter 4 – Easy to Handle... 19
Chapter 5 – Brave 24
Chapter 6 – No Longer Waiting in the Car 29
Chapter 7 – Love.. 36
Chapter 8 – The Sanctuary 41
Chapter 9 – The Forecast Was Wrong or Was It?................. 48
Chapter 10 – Friend Advisor 54
Chapter 11 – Generational Rain.. 58
Chapter 12 – Where is your Umbrella?................................... 62
Chapter 13 – Yes, I'm Talking to Myself................................. 65
Chapter 14 – Sugar Melts in the Rain 70
Chapter 15 – Hydroplaning 73
Chapter 16 – Today, I Sat and Cried 78
Chapter 17 – Feel it Now or Relive it Later 81

Introduction

Reigning While It's Raining

There are times when it seems like every day has rain in the forecast. The rain never stops and it seems as if the sun never shines. The gloomy, dark sky hovers and the ground gives way to the direction of the rain. Just as the environment responds accordingly, I have found that we too respond to rain. Rain has the ability to uproot and settle. For some rain is a soother; for others, rain brings about a feeling of discontentment and depression. In this journal, I want to take life experiences and show you how Reigning While It's Raining is possible!

Chapter 1

I Can't Get My Hair Wet

So, I am natural but I also love me a good weave from time to time. When I see rain instantly I think of what type of hair I have at that moment and how the rain will affect my hair. Silly, but hey I am sure I am not the only one! The feeling of not wanting to get my hair wet makes me think of our reluctance to changing our mindset. In this case, we'll think of our hair as our mindset. For most women, we take pride in our hair. We wait to see if people will notice anything different about it. We relish in compliments and if you are like me you are always looking for ways to change it up. When we find something, we like and feel the most confident with, we wear it a little longer and more often. Then there are those times when people critique us and we start to look at it differently, we may not like it as much or embrace it as much as we did in the beginning.

We become comfortable in our mindset and we park there. We refuse to get "our hair wet". I too struggle with change sometimes. I find that it is easier for me to do what I have always done rather than take a chance at something new, different. I relax in doing the things I have mastered and allow my creativity to become just pages in a journal amongst hundreds of scribbled pages and unfinished plans. Then there are days that I feel like I can brave the rain. My hair being wet won't mean the end of my day or the alteration in the beauty of who I truly am.

Most recently I have spent a lot of time looking inwardly and reflecting on times when I should have and could have made different and sometimes better decisions. I should have braved the rain. I should have embraced the rain in my hair and the opportunity to grow. As a natural, I embrace a good leave-in-conditioner and some room temperature water. I have learned that a little water makes the hair more pliable. In the same sense, I see change as rain. I may not want it to interrupt my day but I do need it from time to time. Change is often feared but there is that acceptance in our mind that we tend to adopt faster than our actions can adjust.

> I just told myself that I would no longer sell myself short.

How do we turn plans into action? We simply just do it! I took a deep breath one day and I just told myself that I would no longer sell myself short. I know that that reference is cliché' but I knew what it meant for me. I simply needed to stop holding back and second-guessing my abilities. I started by professing some positive affirmations daily and even started standing in the mirror (bare-faced) proclaiming my existence and my purpose over myself. The more I changed my mindset about me, the more I was able to "get out of myself" and do things. This journal being one of the things that I "just did". I have said for years that I wanted to do this but I let fear and naysayers discourage me. My leap to do this is a prime example of changing my mind about what I know I am capable of and "just doing".

Let's chat:
- What things have you wrote down that you know you should have completed or should be doing?
- Why have you kept your guard up against the rain, growth?
- What are some ways that you can become consistent with your goals and aspirations?
- Are you willing to let go of your guard and armor and fight for yourself and not against yourself?

Positive Affirmations
- I am capable of fulfilling my dreams and visions
- I am aware of my surroundings and how my life adds value to those around me
- I am not fearful of change or moving forward
- I am eager to work for myself and to still render help to those assigned to me
- I am wise with my time and my abilities

Chapter 2

How I See Me

"You're so pretty to be a dark skin girl", "Your lips are so full, you know people pay for lips like that", "Oh your hair is so thick, do you really like it like that?" and the list goes on with questions and "compliments" that other people offer me. It wasn't until I was asked in my early 20's what I thought about myself outside of what other people had told me. I was sure that I could blurt out at least 10 things that I knew I liked about me. I said things like, my smile (of course the dimples are a plus, thanks mommy), my curves, my skin tone – because I love being chocolate, my public speaking, my love for my children, my commitment to family, my accomplishments, my, my, my well I went blank. I was like wait, how many is that? I was shocked and the lady asking had a smirk. I instantly thought this was a trick question and kept looking for the remainder of my list, I needed three more things. Now, I am sure many of you will be like ahh that's easy. I could name way more than ten. Well, here is the thing. I knew what I had grown to like that others had complimented about me. I knew the things that I was good at, so I leaned in in those areas. But what I did not know, or had not taken the time to explore, was the things that made me who I am without the validation of others. Did I really think that I was a good mother or was I reliant on the affirmation of other mothers who watched me? Was I really confident in my body? Considering all the new fad diets and shakes and whatever else I had tried. Did I really understand how well I spoke and how anointed I was to talk? Looking back, I am forced to answer truthfully, and that answer is no. I was not aware of who I was or what I REALLY had to offer or what I REALLY liked about me.

You see, how you see you is what roots and grounds you for moments of success even when everything around you folds. It wasn't until I started to experience life more that I realized what I thought about me were the things and feelings that would sustain me in any storm or attempted character assassination. And to help I even took the compliments I received and found validation within myself. Do I really like my lips? Am I really a great mother? I found ways within my own scope and understanding to validate those very statements.

> How you see you is what roots and grounds you for moments of success.

Am I saying decline compliments and affirmations? No! I am encouraging you to know you! Compliments should be affirming and not a means of self-discovery. How you see yourself is so important. Learning more about you will help better develop relationships, establish healthy boundaries, effectively execute dreams and visions, When I dug deep and learned more about me, I was able to practice better self-control, efficient goal planning and adequate execution of my plans and visions. I became more pliable. I have to admit that learning and loving you may require some deep digging and some tears, but the results yield a wholeness that is unexplainable.

Dig deep!

I love my _____

because _____

I love the way I _____

because _____

I really like that I _____

because _____

I appreciate my ability to _____

because _____

I am good at _____

so I can _____

I am good at _____

so I can _____

Continue this list.

Chapter 3

Go Against the Grain

Do you remember being told not to jump in the puddle or to be sure to avoid wearing sandals in the rain? When I had my first daughter, I remember telling her those very same things. One day while she and her sister were at one of their Tt's house, they were allowed to not only walk through the puddle but they were encouraged to jump in them. I got a video call and all I saw was mud and smiles. My first reaction was a blank stare, then as they became overwhelmed with laughter, so did I. My friend told me to get over it and find me a puddle! When the video ended I remember crying. Not because I was mad about their clothes or nicely combed hair, but because I had taught them that simple things weren't enjoyable. I know that not all times are puddles acceptable but I had never allowed them to enjoy them or simply running out in the rain. So the next time it rained I encouraged them to go out and I even joined them.

How is this relevant to reigning? Well, we are taught so many things growing up, both good and unintentional restraints, when do we decide what is good for us and what was only for those seasons of life? I have found myself undoing a lot of things that I learned as a child, not because my parents weren't good parents or my influencers were not great, but because I am an adult now, a woman with more self-awareness and discernment. I must have the freedom and desire to shape my beliefs and feelings about life and most importantly my abilities. Many times we as women have the expectations of so many people around us that we neglect to discover our own abilities. I have learned so much about myself just by taking the time to listen to my heart and follow my own path. I am most grateful for the lessons instilled and morals embedded but I am also thankful that even early on I was encouraged to be whatever I wanted and to always embrace my uniqueness. Being a mom, dating, working, going to school among other tasks sometimes limits our desires to discover individuality and purpose. We oftentimes settle for titles and boxes and we get stuck in those places.

> We oftentimes settle for titles and boxes and we get stuck in those places

I want to encourage you to untie yourself from the expectations and dreams that others have for you. Find your puddle and make the biggest splash you can! Discover what you were born to do. Understand what makes you, you! Value the input and guidance of elders, friends, and mentors but establish what it is that you see in you!

List some false expectations that you have lived up to that you realize you should let go of.

_____
_____
_____
_____
_____

Are you holding on to the affirmations of others versus the feelings and thoughts that you have about yourself? If so, why?

_____
_____
_____
_____
_____
_____

What or where is your puddle?

_____

_____

_____

_____

_____

How can you reclaim your presence/existence without offending others?

_____

_____

_____

_____

_____

Chapter 4

Easy to Handle

I think the title of this conversation can be a little deceiving. Most people, especially men will chime in and tell us that we are not easy to handle. Well, sometimes that can be the truth. But are we really easy to handle though? I remember my grandmother telling me whenever I was having a crying spell that tears were good to help you stay pliable on the Potter's wheel. I had not realized how stubborn I was, or as my mother calls me, bullheaded. I had taken on more in life than I could bargain for or with. Mother of two, divorcee and trying to repair what I then called life. I was broken. I was so lost and pretended to be better than I was before all of the changes. I would go home and cry at night. Squeeze my pillow and pray that my sobbing wouldn't wake my girls. I knew that I had made mistakes and that I needed a change in my heart and mind but I wanted to hold onto that hurt for a while. It gave me leverage with the people who had hurt me. I did not like the pain but I had grown accustomed to it. I had taken it as part of my DNA. It wasn't until I started counseling that I realized I was crippling myself more than those who had inflicted the pain. I was able to talk about the things that once held me silent. I was free in my mind and I was getting free in spirit as well. After one of my sessions, my counselor told me to stay pliable to change. Pliable, I had heard that before. That was the same encouragement that my grandmother gave me. I looked the word up again and again just to be sure that I understood what it meant and not just what I thought it meant. I spent time studying the term and pointing out areas in my life that

I had allowed to grow hard without room to be massaged and changed. I have made it a point to examine me more. I am not perfect and still find reasons to examine myself and stay pliable daily.

What areas have you blocked off? Are you afraid to address the things that have you bound and captive to hurt and pain? Spend some time with yourself and maybe include a trustworthy accountability partner. Determine how you can live a life of fullness by letting go of hurts and disappointments.

> I am not perfect and still find reasons to examine myself and stay pliable daily.

Questions to help:

- Are you ready to let go?
- How will letting go affect your future?
- Are you capable of being honest with yourself to receive full freedom?
- What does pliable mean to you?

Chapter 5

Brave

When I think of brave, I think of the women of Wakanda. Before that movie, I thought of Michelle Obama and before her, I thought of individuals who overcame any adversity and wasn't afraid to show their scabs. I remember being so afraid to start Purpose Pushers, LLC. I told myself every day that women already had enough encouragement and I would be just another voice. I would argue with my friend-advisor (I'll explain later) about ideas and how afraid I was. She saw something in my dream and vision but I had allowed fear and anxiety to shift my 20/20 vision of my own goals. Most of the women that I have a chance to talk to whether it be personal or professional admit that they have journals and business plans that have a home, only on paper. They have neglected to bring their ideas to life because of the same reason I addressed - fear. Bravery is defined by Webster as, - the quality or state of having or showing mental or moral strength to face danger, fear, or difficulty: the quality or state of being brave: courage. I like that the definition expresses that danger, difficulty and fear exist within bravery but it first establishes that there is STRENGTH to overcome all of the aforementioned. So get excited if you are experiencing any fear, danger, or difficulty – you have the opportunity to exercise your bravery! You got this sis. Dig deep! Put on your big girl panties as they say and your good rain boots and purpose forward! You are equipped to win. I want to share with you some

> You got this sis.
>
> Dig deep!

positive affirmations that help me in times where fear screams louder than I would like.

My ideas have the right to live!

Fear will not cripple me, it will fuel me to push harder.

I am destined to succeed!

I have all that I need to become and do all that I am destined to see and execute!

If I must fear it will be fear of complacency!

I will always consider my future when making present decisions.

I speak kindly to myself and am patient with my progress.

I understand that bravery is not a bulldozer.

I operate with compassion while still setting healthy and obtainable goals.

Make some declarations over yourself!

Chapter 6
No Longer Waiting in the Car

I do not care where I had to be and what was going on, if rain came, I would be forced to stay in my car and wait for it to "slack up". So, you get it, the rain stopped me and, in a sense, trapped me. I was used to comfort and staying dry. I did not want to deal with the extra steps needed to dry off. The fact that I am short also means that majority of the time my pant legs would be drenched if I wasn't prepared. I would spend the time in the car listening to the radio, scrolling Facebook, cleaning out my purse, but ultimately taking time away from the task that I should be completing. I was headed to a meeting one day and it began to rain really hard. I knew automatically that I was going to wait in my car since I was a little early anyway. I remember just staring off into the rain-splattered windshield with no thought. No worry or direction. But then I started to realize how sitting in that car when I could have taken the time spent in the car preparing and actually taking advantage of the meet and greet. This journal entry was birthed from that experience. I realized how trapped I was sitting in comfort. I was comfortable with being in what I saw as a safe place. In reality, sometimes our place of comfort isn't safe, it's dry. We become complacent. We wit in our cars and we wait for the perfect moment. We wait for what we think is the best time. I am guilty. I have hypothetically waited in my car more times than I should have. I have sat in comfort and waited in dry places more than I should have. Comfort is great for times when we have worked to that place not when we have built that place as a barrier or shelter. I chose at some point on this journey to relinquish comfort and pursue my purpose unapologetically. It was a little different at first but then I found peace in no longer waiting in the car. I seized moments of networking, goal setting, and purpose pushing to be so much more fulfilling than "waiting in the car". Dry barren places are places that lack the means of production. I started professing and claiming that my life was more than a comfort zone for fear and complacency.

> It was a little different at first but then I found peace in no longer waiting in the car.

What has you stuck in your car?

_____
_____
_____
_____
_____

How can you take those things and fuel your purpose?

_____
_____
_____
_____
_____

Are you too comfortable?

What are three ways that you can avoid complacency?

Reigning While It's Raining

What pushes you to a dry and barren place?

_____
_____
_____
_____
_____

Are you willing to leave the hindrances behind and get out of the car?

_____
_____
_____
_____
_____

Chapter 7
Love

I instantly started singing, A word that comes and goes but few people really know what it means... lol! I still wonder how this four-letter word has so much power. It has so many definitions. It is both assuring and disturbing. It is confident and yet sometimes so questionable. The Bible says that it is patient and kind. It covers. It promotes. Love to me is one of those things that is ever-evolving. It changes day by day. It grows and diminishes with time. I dare to even think of one definition that best suits this entry. I want to say that love of self is how I want to highlight my friend, love. Learning to love is a journey of discovery. Mistakes made and triumphs celebrated. Love makes the lips turn to a smirk and sometimes a full smile. It also has the ability to provoke one simple tear. Love is what drives us, and, often, we don't follow the directions. Love is comforting and reminds of nostalgic instances. Love can also recant fear and second guesses. Love is never complete in the sense that it is ever-changing. Love brings about change and suggests ways to accept happiness and peace. It is never predictable and can always be found even in the subtlest ways. I want to state that I think love is… It just is. Now if you're emotional like me you are likely crying by now. Love floods me with so many emotions. There is one thing that I notice all women can say about love, it can be tricky. We have all been hurt at some point whether in relationships, family, professionally, and even sometimes we've hurt ourselves. Can I challenge you to rediscover love? Are

> Can I challenge you to rediscover love?

you willing to look beyond what you have been taught? Are you willing to make your own decision about love with clear and precise attention? Are you willing to fight and break barriers? Are you willing to love and be loved?

This is your love page.

No prompts.

No questions.

Just you and love!

Chapter 8

The Sanctuary

Now, this is a lesson that I am still learning myself, but it is so refreshing to share the experiences with you. I remember my grandmother always telling me that not everyone deserved to come in her kitchen. Her kitchen was her sacred place. Great things were produced there. She spent time praying over her family there. She wrote her plans and visions in notebooks that were stored on a table in that little kitchen. My brother and I would run in from outside and tug her black, skin-so-soft scented slip in anticipation for some cold Kool-Aid and maybe even a snack. She would warn us to get out of her kitchen but all the while meeting our requests. We thought that the kitchen was just for grown-ups until we learned that the kitchen was granny's sanctuary. This was her safe place. She had cultivated a presence in her kitchen that brought not only peace but increased clarity of her thoughts and feelings. She could face her stove and all we knew was something smelled great but she would be praying and wiping her tears. We would see her seated separating peas into a small bowl of water but really, she was counting her blessings and focused on what was ahead. You see the kitchen was more than just her kitchen. Now that I am older, I have grown to love the idea of having my own sanctuary. For me, it is my shower. My girls know that when I turn off the lights and leave only a candle flicker that I am in my sanctuary. Now I get that this may sound like

> All we knew was something smelled great but she would be praying and wiping her tears

cliché woman relaxation but for me stepping out of my day and behind that curtain brings me a peace, a release. This is the place where I become vulnerable to my feelings and emotions. I am unashamed. I am aware of myself and not distracted by anything or anyone. The feeling behind the curtain that I feel is unexplainable. I have other places that I retreat to but this to me is a lot like granny's kitchen. And not every visit to the shower is a sanctuary visit. I have learned to discern when that time is needed. As women, we must find places that we are able to release. Places that take our energy – good, bad, ugly or cute and give it back to us in the purest form. A place where we are surrounded by security and assurance. You may ask how in the world did she find that in her shower? Well, I cultivated it just like my granny did. I made that place mine. Sure, others use it but when I am in it, it becomes what I need it to be, my sanctuary.

What does the word sanctuary mean to you?

_____

_____

_____

_____

_____

Where is your safe place, your sanctuary?

_____

_____

_____

_____

_____

How important is finding a sanctuary to you?

_____

_____

_____

_____

_____

Are you willing to cultivate a place of safety for you that no one can alter?

_____

_____

_____

_____

_____

Do you realize your need for a safe place?

_____
_____
_____
_____
_____

I absolutely hate when I check the forecast and then the day does not end up the way it was forecasted. I prepare for 80 degrees and in Alabama, by lunch, it may be 67 degrees and then by the end of the workday it might be 94 degrees. I expect one thing and get another. Life and people are the same way. The one thing that I think all mothers share with their children, is that not everyone is your friend. I use to roll my eyes and mumble, "how do you know" (don't tell my momma she'll still try to pop me lol). Now I understand all too well. I have learned that what I think and see in people may be wrong or at least what I see is not yet manifested. I struggle with believing that people intentionally seek to be malicious and unfair in friendships. Over the years I have learned about incorrect forecasts in relationships be it personal or professional. Life too has a way of yielding incorrect forecasts. I prepare

> I have learned that false expectations are easily grown and sometimes watered too often.

for one thing and another happens. I have learned that false expectations are easily grown and sometimes watered too often. So, the questions are, was the forecast wrong or was the expectation off? The weatherman can say, "hey prepare for 80-degree weather and a feel of 67 with a windchill" and all we heard was 80-degree weather. I have formed an opinion about something or someone, hence a forecast and it turns out I was sometimes wrong. I had the wrong perception or wrong introduction. Sometimes we perceive things based off of someone else's experiences, we cheat ourselves by doing this. So, I guess all in all what I am trying to say is this, be mindful of expectations and perceptions. Be fair and reasonable in communications and discernment. I have learned that getting a feel for things and people on my own makes a difference in my expectations. Discernment is key and yields fruitful relationships.

Have you ever been persuaded in your forecast of people or things and feel that you missed out because of it?

_____
_____
_____
_____
_____

How can you heighten your discernment?

_____
_____
_____
_____
_____

Are you willing to admit that sometimes you are wrong about people based on your own false expectations?

_____
_____
_____
_____
_____

Chapter 10
Friend Advisor

So, I told you that we would talk about this earlier in the journal. I have had a chance to meet some really, really amazing women in life. Some of these women are friends I have had since elementary school, some I have just come to know and love and a few have fallen away. I have found that not all friendships are alike and the older I get the more I appreciate the diversity in my friendships. It was more recent that I came to appreciate the friends that were also advisors. Now we all look to our friends for advice from time to time but to find that some of these friends are better at holding you accountable in certain areas than others is amazing! I know which friend is right for each situation. I genuinely know and affirm that they all love me but they each have their own specialty and also their way of dealing with me. I have learned that those who I consider to be my friend-advisors are the friends that see my vision but they see it completed and full. They are eager for me to move beyond the talk-about-it phase. They do not offer me a pity party on my 'I don't feel like it days' and they are constant reminders of the deadlines that they have set for me. I hope that you are surrounded by friends who are great friend-advisors to you. I want to encourage you to remind those same friends of their visions and dreams. Remind them that they are important and their help is more than appreciated. Take them along on your journey and never allow anyone or anything to discredit that relationship. While

> I know which friend is right for each situation.

they are pushing you, I employ you to do the same for them. I have learned that many of my friend-advisors are great background pushers. They prefer not to be out front. They are happiest with pushing and not being pushed. Not because they have nothing going on or because they don't have dreams but because they are nurturers by nature and they get joy from helping. Be their joy too! Push and pull! Friendship is an even exchange.

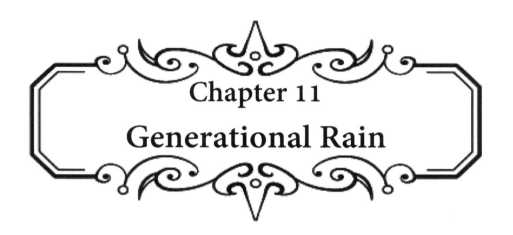

Chapter 11
Generational Rain

I remember a classmate of mine in college telling me that she felt that her whole bloodline was tainted. She felt like depression and poverty was all they knew, no matter how hard they worked. I was taught early on about generational curses and how things are genetically passed down. I would pray with her and encourage her but the one thing I did not do was challenge her. It may seem like a generational torrential rain never ends and getting up is nearly impossible. I am of the belief that had I moved beyond words and challenged my classmate we would have experienced different results. You are not mandated to be like momma nem'. Granted science has a suggestion about genetics but the beautiful thing about rain it that it has multiple perceptions. It can bring life and, in some cases, it can hinder or stall plans. I want to suggest that we take generational rains and declare that for us this torrential rain provides a cleansing and we have the right and ability to rid ourselves of negligent acceptance. We do not have to just take or accept behaviors, attitudes, and statuses because everyone in the family has accepted any of those. The greatest thing about rain is that it provides a means for growth. See the adversity and decide that the rain for you will not stop you from reigning! You will be cleansed and renewed. Nothing holds you back from your destiny like self-doubt and

> The greatest thing about rain is that it provides a means for growth.

fear. Relinquish control and let the rain help you release so that you can reign!

Chapter 12

Where is Your Umbrella?

Sometimes I figure that it is easier for me to just run without my umbrella. The hassle of digging in my trunk for it or untangling a doll that my youngest has hid in it seems like too much work until I am running in the rain at what seems like the pace of a snail. I end up drenched and likely frustrated. But, for some reason, I am willing to try the method again and again. More recently I started keeping a smaller more compact umbrella lodged between my driver seat and console. No more excuses. I realized that I needed my umbrella to be readily accessible. I needed my covering! So many times, in life I have taken the convenient (or what seemed to be a convenient) route and ended up frustrated. In a more literal sense, who covers you? Are you roaming alone with trust issues and suspicions? Are you gathering negative thoughts about your ability to trust and be trusted? Do you have a covering that is both uplifting and corrective? For some, this covering may be a Pastoral, mentoring, or simply your accountability to your tribe. Trusting yourself with others for your benefit will result in growth. As much as society would like to tell us that we do not need other people, the truth is, we do!

> As much as society would like to tell us that we do not need other people, the truth is, we do!

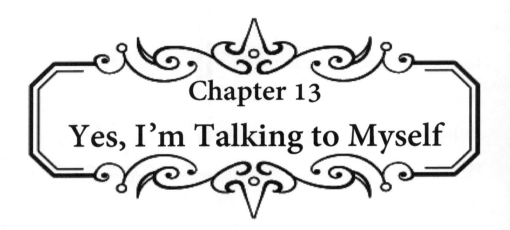

Chapter 13

Yes, I'm Talking to Myself

I remember being a little girl and always hearing, if you talk to yourself, you're crazy. As I grew up it changed to, you can talk to yourself but don't answer. I remember being in my African American Studies class at Alabama State University my freshman year, and my instructor made a statement I will never forget. He told us that if we aren't having regular conversations with ourselves, we are doing ourselves and our future a great disservice. He explained that conversations with yourself should be both provoking and empowering. That small lesson or as he would call it, "debt-free advice" changed my perspective on how I communicate with myself.

The time we spend listening to others and soliciting their opinions and thoughts can be helpful but how we speak to ourselves is just as important. I remember being afraid of talking to myself, simply being alone with myself. I had a breaking point and realized that I had not handled myself with care. I was breezing through life and had not fed myself from my own love bank. I relied on affirmation and support from family and friends. I needed to embrace me and love me. I needed to feel and know the love of self. I begin to have morning chats with myself. I would repeat positive affirmations and then took it a step further and started to walk myself through events and happenings that had detoured me from taking care of me. I talked and I

> I love compliments but they aren't necessary for me to feel pretty or worthy.

responded. I needed this. I did not make this a means of escape from outward consistent communication but I did form a relationship with me that was empowering and reassuring. I love compliments but they aren't necessary for me to feel pretty or worthy. I love company but it isn't necessary for me to enjoy my outing. I became comfortable with me and my life changed, for the better.

Just your time!

Spend some time alone within the next 30 days. Plan a date that you enjoy and leave your phone home.

Set purposed time each day to speak over your life in a positive manner.

Go through your memory bank and talk yourself through some of that built up anguish and hurt.

Take 5 minutes a day and look in the mirror. No makeup. No distractions.

Encourage another sister to do these with you and hold each other accountable.

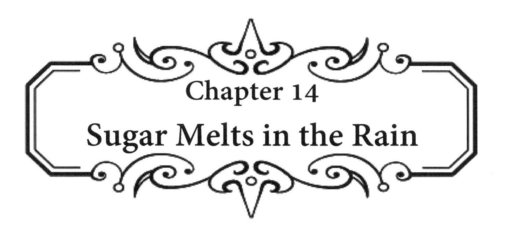

I loved it when I would run into my grandparent's house when it was raining and my granddaddy would say, "You must think you sugar, sugar melts in the rain." I would blush of course. But I did think I was cute lol! Truth is sugar does melt in the rain. In a more literal sense our "sweetness", kindness sometimes wears off easily when we are drenched in adversity or uncomfortableness. We attempt to shake it off and purpose on but truth is.. over time we are not as sweet as we would like to be. My grandmother would respond to my granddaddy with, "She is sugar but she bet not ever melt." She was the one that encouraged me always to be me. Be sweet! Never let circumstance or situations alter who you are and always choose to sprinkle your touch. Have you been hurt or let down and felt like you needed to lessen your sweetness? Well, that is unfair to yourself for starters. You deserve the right to be the very essence of who you were created to be regardless of what anyone else thinks or feels! Life has a way of humbling us and growing us but never should it diminish us. Have you allowed an experience to water down your sweetness? Are you still encouraged to help and be soft when necessary? Identify ways to protect your sweetness!

> Life has a way of humbling us and growing us but never should it diminish us.

Chapter 15
Hydroplaning

In Driver's Education, I remember us talking about hydroplaning and I also remember stories from people who had hydroplaned, but no amount of teaching or discussion can prepare you for your personal experience with hydroplaning. By definition (Wikipedia) hydroplaning is a result of water builds up between the wheels of the vehicle which causes the car to lose traction. Have you ever felt that your current situation has caused you to in a sense hydroplane? Are you unsure of how to brace yourself for what seems to be the out of control results? Sometimes in life, we will find that hydroplaning is not such a bad thing after all. We need to relinquish control.

> We need to relinquish control.

Sometimes losing control is the best way to rebuild control. Sure, there are risks and potential dangers in hydroplaning but when faced with danger or risks we usually resurface with a greater appreciation for life and the things around us. After the scare and regroup what do you do? Have you experienced any area of your life where you felt that you were hydroplaning? Have you recovered? How did/do you recover?

Steps to Regaining Control
- Accepting where you are without comparison to where you think you should be
- Setting realistic goals based on what's within reach

- Spend time with yourself
- Invest in your life and goals
- Relinquish false responsibilities
- Establish healthy boundaries
- Believe in yourself and yourself with care

Water is water no matter what form. It conforms but persists to transform. Mirages distract you until reality grasps you. Dampened by happenings, soaked in recovery. Drowning with open mouths. Saved by expanded lungs and released fight. Splashing brings freedom. Stifled creations make for a woeful heart and broken spirit. Thinking you can, means that ultimately, YOU WILL. Fear is just as scared as you are. It is just happy with having a place to live. Dreaming doesn't require sleep, it requires belief. Sweet, caring, loving, kind. You decide to what measure. Belonging is simple when you are amongst those to which you belong. Tribe finding. Your future is not waiting for you to arrive it is waiting for you to begin living. Your limits are not really limiting they are only fears that have set up boundaries to your future. Your silence is unfair to the younger you that was told you can do and be anything you set your mind to. Bloom where you are planted and you will always be nourished.

Chapter 16
Today, I Sat and Cried

I am overwhelmed sometimes with emotions about life, the happenings, the things that I want to happen but are yet to manifest, the experiences, just life. I use to be super emotional when I was younger. I would cry and write poetry anytime something bothered me and sometimes they were tears of joy and the writings had a happier rhythm. My family was never one to tell me that crying was for weak people. I have met many people that were deprived of crying moments because they associated tears with weakness. Honestly, tears have proven to be some of my most empowering moments. I have been able to begin a cry in sorrow, anguish or anger but end with strategy and fulfillment to push past whatever the obstacle may be. When was the last time you cried? Do you know that God has a record of our tears (Psalms 56:8)? This means tears are fruitful in some regards. Are you all cried out? Have you reached a season where tears are your normal language? If you have neglected to allow yourself to cry I want to encourage you to find your moment. I bet some of you are like, wait, so I need to just sit and cry for no reason? Well, honestly, yes! Too many times I looked for a reason to release what I had already experienced. I simply needed to yield to myself and my emotions! I am challenging you to yield to yourself and your emotions! Find your moment!

> I am challenging you to yield to yourself and your emotions!

Chapter 17

Feel it Now or Relive it Later

I was 25 years old, mother of one daughter, pregnant with my second daughter, going through a divorce and really just lost. I was quiet during this season of my life. I was so glad when summer came that year. This meant that my oldest daughter would start her time away from home with her grandparents, her dad and any other adventures that came. I needed and wanted to just be in bed. I wanted to hide. I wanted to simply wake up and all this be done and over. I had no clue what I was going through exactly but I knew I did not like the feeling so I had become numb to a lot of it. It was one morning my grandmother called me and told me to sit up (she knew I loved my bed) and listen carefully. She told me that I needed to feel all that I was enduring now so that I wouldn't have to feel it to this magnitude later. I wept and wept. She told me that if this circled again, I wouldn't feel the need to be angry I will have a sense of understanding and handle it with care rather than regret. That was one of the most prized pieces of advice that she shared with me. I continue sharing that information with anyone that I have the opportunity to chat with when they are enduring hard times. So many times, I think we chose to skip the process and go straight to the end result. Life has a cycle and so do our issues and situations. Skipping any parts of the process leads to unnecessary

> Skipping any parts of the process leads to unnecessary repetition.

repetition. Feeling it while you're in it allows for new perspectives and discoveries. You have a chance to analyze and actually respond from that vantage point rather than peeling a scab later. Feel it now, build on the recovery and testimony for later.

Reigning While It's Reigning

*A Woman's Journey
Towards Her Destiny*